The dashing Prince Constantine, an Olympic Gold medallist and heir to the Greek throne, was one of the world's most eligible bachelors when he fell in love with a young Danish Princess in 1962. When they married, two years later, Constantine was King, and their glittering state wedding promised a glorious future for the monarchy. But political changes caused Constantine to lose his throne and the couple lived out their love story in exile

♛ *The young Crown Prince Constantine holds a fine white cockerel during a visit to a Greek poultry farm. The picture was taken several years after the family's return to Greece*

LANDS APART

A GREEK PRINCE AND A DANISH PRINCESS GREW UP IN DIFFERENT LANDS BUT, DESPITE INFORMAL UPBRINGINGS, WERE INSTILLED WITH A SENSE OF ROYAL RESPONSIBILITY

P RINCE CONSTANTINE WAS BORN ON Sunday 2 June 1940, the second child of Crown Prince Paul of Greece and his wife, Frederica. The birth took place in the sitting-room of their home at Psychico, a modest villa situated on the outskirts of Athens.

The Crown Prince remained at Frederica's side throughout the labour, holding her hand. Her parents, the Duke and Duchess of Brunswick, had been present at the birth of her first child, Sofia, but the outbreak of war prevented them from assisting with the arrival of Constantine. As was the custom, the Prime Minister and the King – Paul's elder brother – were present in the house, awaiting news.

The birth was trouble-free and, in a rare show of feeling, King George embraced his brother warmly. Shortly before 6 p.m., a salute of 101 guns boomed out from Mount Lycabettus, announcing to Athenians the addition to the Royal Family. Six weeks later, Constantine was baptized in Athens Cathedral.

Wartime evacuation

These moments of joy were rapidly eclipsed by the stark realities of war. The Greek army fared well in their opening encounters with the Italian forces but, when German units launched an offensive from Bulgaria in April

♛ *A group picture of the Greek Royal Family, taken in 1947, shortly after King Paul's accession to the throne. With King Paul and Queen Frederica are Crown Prince Constantine, aged six, Princess Irene, aged four and, seated on the wall, Princess Sofia, aged eight. They are in the garden of their home at Psychico. King Paul, who wears a naval uniform, was a very keen sailor*

1941, the Greek position swiftly deteriorated. Bombs shook the airfield and the port of Athens. It was decided that Frederica and the children should be evacuated to Crete.

There, the family was scarcely safer. During one air raid, they were forced to take refuge in an open ditch. The Royal nurse, Sheila McNair, gripped the baby Constantine tightly while Frederica tried to comfort her daughter by singing 'Baa, baa, black sheep'.

From Crete, the Royal party moved on to Egypt, where Frederica found to her consternation that the children had developed ugly, red rashes from bug and flea bites. Even so, the tranquility of Alexandria seemed hard to believe after the wartime conditions in Greece. But the city proved a temporary haven only. Their presence was an embarrassment to King Farouk's government and they were soon obliged to depart.

Frequent moves

In the event, Frederica and her children spent the remainder of World War II in South Africa, while her husband, Crown Prince Paul, accompanied the King to London, to continue the war effort. During the next five years, Frederica and the children changed home 22 times, often staying in cheap hotels that were dilapidated or rat-infested.

In spite of these disruptions, family morale was high. Frederica was fortunate in gaining the friendship and support of the South African Premier, Jan Smuts, who became the godfather of her third child, Irene, who was born in May 1942. Little Tino – Constantine's nickname – showed no sign of being affected by the upheavals, and he would listen out avidly for his father's voice on the radio, refusing to go to bed without kissing the

Constantine enjoys the humour of the situation as he poses with one of the Royal palace guards. Both are wearing Evzone costume, a traditional Greek costume worn by the elite Greek infantry regiment

Popperfoto

Constantine reads aloud to his form-mates in one of the classrooms at Anavryta College in Kifissia below left. He started at this new school when he was aged eight. In the grounds of Tatoi Palace below right Constantine takes the wheel of a jeep with his young sisters as passengers

Crown Prince's photograph goodnight.

The family were reunited in Egypt in 1944, but were unable to return to Greece until after the elections in 1946. The war was over and they found a country torn apart by poverty and civil strife. Communist bands waged a full-scale guerrilla campaign until the end of the decade. In the meantime, Paul had ascended to the throne, following the death of King George II in April 1947. The six-year-old Constantine's first public duty as the new Crown Prince was to accompany his father in the funeral procession in Athens Cathedral.

World News, Athens

World News, Athens

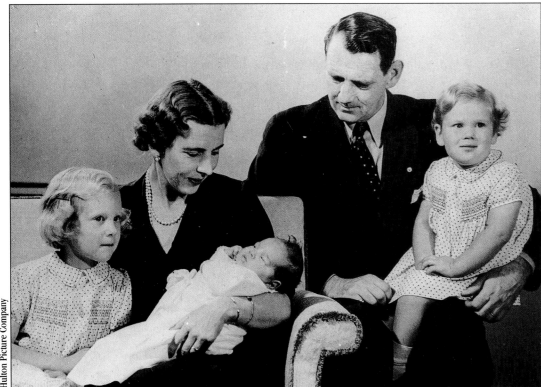

Hulton Picture Company

♛ A picture taken in October 1946 of the baby Princess Anne-Marie with her family left. The occasion was her christening in Copenhagen, when she was given the names Anne-Marie Dagmar Ingrid. The baby is in the arms of her mother, Crown Princess Ingrid, and sitting beside her on the sofa is Princess Margrethe, the eldest of the Royal children. Crown Prince Frederik looks on with Princess Benedikte on his knee

Hulton Picture Company

Denmark, too, suffered heavily during the war. The country was occupied by the Germans in April 1940 but its Royal Family were able to remain with their people throughout the hostilities. King Christian X used to ride through the streets of Copenhagen whenever possible, trying to keep alive the national spirit of independence.

The Danish Royal Family

The morale of the Danish Royal Family, like that of their Greek counterparts, was boosted by the arrival of new children. Crown Prince Frederik and his wife Ingrid had three daughters. The eldest, Margrethe, was born a week after the German invasion, Princess Benedikte was born in 1944 and Anne-Marie followed on August 30 1946, soon after the liberation of her country. In another curious parallel with Greece, Anne-Marie's father was crowned King in April 1947, the same month in which Constantine's father became King of the Hellenes.

The informal Danes

The Danish monarchy had its roots in the house of Oldenborg, the oldest Royal line in Europe. Its pedigree is traced back to 1448. Yet, despite its antiquity, the family has fostered a style of informality that has served as a model for other European monarchies.

Anne-Marie's father, Frederik IX, was the epitome of a citizen-king. A giant of a man, passionately interested in music and sailing, he endeared himself to his subjects by the

♛ On a visit to London in June 1952 Princess Anne-Marie, aged six, experiences the fun – and the fear – of the helter-skelter at Battersea Festival Pleasure Gardens. She is accompanied by a lady-in-waiting. Anne-Marie visited the funfair with her sister Benedikte, the Duchess of Gloucester and Prince Richard of Gloucester

♛ King Frederik top right greets his eager daughters on the quayside at Copenhagen, after a voyage in the Royal yacht Dannebrog. Margrethe, half hidden, is hugging him and Anne-Marie is leaping up for a kiss. Benedikte impatiently waits her turn and the Queen looks on with pleasure. Queen Ingrid right below on board ship with the three Princesses

Hulton Picture Company

Hulton Picture Company

charming habit of referring to the Queen and himself in public speeches as 'Mother and I'. In a similar vein, Queen Ingrid was content to wait in queues for service when out shopping and the entire family were happy to be seen out riding on their bicycles.

The Danes also did much to popularize the Royal walkabout. From the start of their reign, Frederik and Ingrid were keen to mingle freely with their subjects on public occasions, employing a minimum of security. Frederik actually caused a stir during one of his visits to England in the 1950s by making an unscheduled stop to exchange a few pleasantries with a train driver and his fireman. The British Press were shocked at this lack of reserve, although by the 1990s it would seem entirely natural behaviour for a member of the Royal Family. There were also regular reports of foreign tourists strolling through the Tivoli Gardens in Copenhagen and striking up a conversation with a friendly stranger, and finding to their surprise that they were talking to the King of Denmark.

Relaxed upbringing

Anne-Marie grew up in this relaxed and happy atmosphere, a gay, confident child, scarcely aware that she was being spared many of the worst inconveniences of having a Royal background. She was able to enjoy a good deal of privacy, with few restrictions on her movements, and grew up in much the same way as would an ordinary child.

As part of a close-knit family, it was inevitable that some of Anne-Marie's earliest public appearances should have been on domestic occasions. In particular, she took part as a child in the annual celebration of the King's birthday on 11 March when, by tradition, the entire Royal Family appeared on the balcony to wave at the thousands who gathered in Amalienborg Palace Square.

Anne-Marie and her sisters were seldom separated from their parents. Frederik liked to turn the Royal visits to various parts of the country into family occasions, and he also made a point of spending tea-time with his wife and daughters, if official duties permitted. He once paid a public tribute to the four of them, describing them as 'the lucky clover-leaf that has brought happiness into my life and sunshine streaming into my heart.'

There was a distinctly English atmosphere about Anne-Marie's home life. Her nurse had been Mary North, the daughter of Admiral Sir Dudley North and, throughout her childhood, Queen Ingrid ensured that she and her sisters had English companions, so that they would learn to speak the language fluently. Anne-Marie visited England several times before her

5

marriage and, on one of these trips, she accompanied her father to Folkestone, to watch him present new colours to the Royal Kent Regiment of the Queen's Own Buffs, of which he was Colonel-in-Chief.

The English influence was carried through into education. Both of Anne-Marie's sisters were sent to English public schools and Princess Margrethe went on to attend courses at Girton College, Cambridge and the London School of Economics. It came as a surprise when Anne-Marie herself was sent to the Chatelard School, a prestigious finishing-school near Montreux in Switzerland.

After the lack of ostentation at her conventional high school near Copenhagen, this move abroad was upsetting and, at first, Anne-Marie was very homesick. However, she eventually settled down, making friends and enjoying the typical teenage pursuits of fashion and pop music. What she found hardest to adapt to was the lack of privacy and the way she could no longer wander freely around the local shops without becoming the centre of attention.

Greece's Crown Prince

Constantine, for his part, was an easy-going boy, unruffled by crowds and quick with a mischievous smile. But he was also capable of a serious mien which his father cultivated gently. From the age of nine, Constantine's education was carefully geared to his future public role. Initially, he studied at the small private school in the old family house at Psychico, which had been vacated after Paul's succession, when the Royal Family moved into the palaces of Athens and Tatoi.

From 1948, however, the Crown Prince attended the newly-founded school of Anavry-

Hulton Picture Company

⚜ *The Danish Royal Family. Princess Benedikte is seated and Anne-Marie is on the right. The picture was taken to mark Benedikte's Confirmation at the Fredensborg Church. Anne-Marie, the youngest of the Royal children, was aged 12 at the time*

ANNE-MARIE'S PALACE

Anne-Marie's childhood home was the picturesque Amalienborg Palace, a rococo gem situated in the centre of Copenhagen. The Palace is a complex of four separate buildings, linked together by colonnades to form the shape of a diamond around an old, cobbled courtyard. The Palace has a faintly English atmosphere as, when the Monarch is in residence, a daily changing of the guard ceremony takes place, performed by soldiers wearing traditional uniforms and bearskins. Anne-Marie was born in the Palace and celebrated her 'coming out' at a party in the magnificent ballroom. The balcony at Amalienborg Palace is the traditional venue for Royal appearances on formal occasions

Topham

Topham

Syndication International

♛ *In the winter of 1958 Anne-Marie and her sisters took their annual skiing holiday* left *on the slopes at Gausdal, Norway, Anne-Marie, seen here at the start of a run, was already a very pretty girl, though still only 12 years old*

♛ *Princess Anne-Marie* right *visited the circus in Copenhagen with her sisters and the young Greek royals when she was aged 12. She immediately fell for Constantine, her handsome 18-year-old third cousin*

ta at Kifissia, ten miles outside Athens. Anavryta was closely based on the famous schools founded by Dr Kurt Hahn at Salem, in southern Germany, and at Gordonstoun. Hahn was an educational guru who wanted to establish a type of school that would build independence, character and a resilience of spirit. The first headmaster of the new school, and Constantine's personal tutor, was Jocelyn Winthrop Young, an ex-pupil of Gordonstoun.

Although treated on an equal footing with other pupils, Constantine had already discovered that independence had, for him, a special meaning. Once, in boyhood, he was refused credit by a shopkeeper in a fishing village to which he had wandered. 'I am the Crown Prince,' he protested. The shopkeeper rang the Palace and King Paul came to collect his hungry, lost son.

Learning with others

At Anavryta, Constantine developed his natural ability both to be informal and to take pride in responsibility. He was photographed stiffly determined in uniform at an academy for military officer cadets which he also attended. As at school, he shared the same dormitories, ate the same food and was subject to the same discipline.

After leaving school, Constantine attended Athens University, studying law, economics and military history, but had to withdraw from his courses when student demonstrations and strikes broke out on the campus. It was deemed unwise for a future King to be associated too closely with these protests. Constantine's studies were completed with private tutors. He took a special course on the basics of nuclear physics.

Paul l King	*m.*	*Frederika, Princess,*		*King Frederick*	*m.*	*Princess Ingrid*
of the Hellenes		*of Hanover*		*of Denmark*		*of Sweden*
(1901-1964)		*(1917-1981)*		*(1899-1972)*		*(b. 1910)*

Sofia	*m.*	*King Juan Carlos*	*Irene*	*Queen Margrethe*	*m.*	*Henri-Marie*	*Benedikta*	*m.*	*Prince Richard*
(b 1938)		*of Spain*	*(b. 1942)*	*(b. 1940)*		*Comte de Laborde*	*(b. 1944)*		*zu Sayn-Wittgenstein*
		(b. 1938)				*de Monpezat*			

King Constantine	*m.*	*Princess Anne-*
(b. 1940)		*Marie of Denmark*
		(b. 1946)

A Danish-Hellenic Union

Alexia	*Paul*	*Nicholas*	*Theodora*	*Philippos*
(b. 1965)	*(b. 1967)*	*(b. 1969)*	*(b. 1983)*	*(b. 1986)*

COMING OF AGE

His very varied training did not dampen the Crown Prince's lively sense of humour which occasionally landed him in some rather unregal situations. Queen Frederica recounted an incident which occurred when her teenage son accompanied her to the United States in 1958. In between official functions, Tino decided to visit his cousin Simeon, the exiled King of Bulgaria. The two young men went for a drive during which they were involved in a minor accident. A police officer appeared and asked to see their papers. As they had none, the policeman demanded to know their identities. 'I am the Crown Prince of Greece,' Constantine replied politely. 'Oh sure! And who is your friend, then?' 'That is my cousin, the King of Bulgaria,' he continued, mischievously, knowing full well that the policeman would never believe him.

Inevitably, the young royalty were locked up in a police van and taken to the station. They were detained, highly amused, until their aides arrived to confirm their story. Such high spirits were, in Constantine, balanced by a shrewd grasp of the complex politics of Greece. But no amount of acumen or school-

Camera Press

♛ *Crown Prince Constantine and his father King Paul I were very close. This charming picture was taken to mark Constantine's 16th birthday. The King, a keen naval man, was unusual among Royals in having a tattoo on his forearm*

♛ *Constantine, who held the ancient title of Duke of Sparta, took part in a Greek tragedy by Sophocles in his last year at Anavryta College. He is seen below in the chorus during a public open-air performance of* Philoctetes

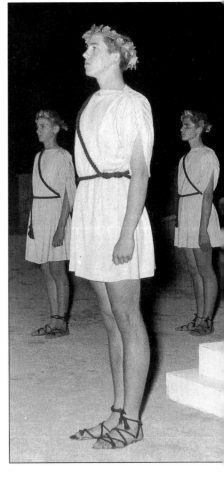

World News, Athens

THE PRINCE'S REFUGE

Constantine's infant years in South Africa were positively nomadic. Far from being a comfortable haven from the war, the country was packed with European refugees and conditions were poor. After losing their possessions in a fire at their first abode, Frederica and the children stayed briefly in 'Groote Schuur', Cecil Rhodes' old house, before finding a more permanent home outside Cape Town, in an old bungalow. The place was infested with rats and cockroaches, and Frederica was scared out of her wits when a donkey unexpectedly popped its head through a window. Eventually, the Royal refugees were rescued by General Smuts *below*, who invited them to stay in his official residence in Pretoria

ing could alone prepare a Prince for the reality of the throne. Accordingly, King Paul had decided to organize this aspect of his son's education himself.

From the age of eleven onwards, Tino was allowed to be present in the King's audience room, while he was involved in conferences or in a working session with one of his government ministers. Initially, the boy was required to keep silent. But, as he grew older, the King would occasionally interrupt the

'Remember that it is preferable that the King should suffer than that the suffering should fall on the nation'

KING PAUL TO CROWN PRINCE CONSTANTINE

meeting to explain some detail to his son and finally, when Constantine reached the age of 18, he was encouraged to make his own contribution to the discussions.

Pledging allegiance to Greece

The fruition of these studies came on 28 June, 1958, when Constantine celebrated his coming-of-age by pledging his oath of allegiance to the King and by accepting his commission as an officer. It was a moving ceremony, held in

⚜ At a farewell ceremony for military cadets, who were leaving Athens for Crete, Constantine took the salute below. The cadets were going to take part in a commemorative battle. This was the 16-year-old Crown Prince's first official function on his own

the Trophy Room of the Parliament building. Everyone was in full dress uniform or evening clothes, and the company included representatives of the government, the armed forces and foreign delegations.

After the playing of the national anthem, King Paul addressed the Crown Prince with some carefully chosen words of advice: 'Be a just, kind and indefatigable worker for the advance and glory of Greece. Uphold steadfastly the Democratic principles ... and constitutional liberties of our People. Devote your life to the happiness of the Country ... Always remember that it is preferable that the King should suffer than that the suffering should fall on the nation.'

Father and son could scarcely look at each other throughout the ceremony, afraid of losing control of their feelings. It was the final stage of Constantine's apprenticeship.

Topham

⚜ When Constantine came of age, in June 1958, he made an official drive through Athens with King Paul and Queen Frederica left. He was now entitled to act as Regent in the absence of his father, the King

Popperfoto

Camera Press

♛ *A lively child, Constantine spent most of his early years abroad*

♛ *Back home in Athens, the Crown Prince tried his hand at gardening*

♛ *Constantine was sent to school at Anavryta to learn the manly virtues and the pleasures of competition*

♛ *In the school holidays, the Prince spent time at home with his sisters Irene and Sofia*

👑 *Anne-Marie, as the youngest child, was born into a ready-made loving family*

👑 *King Frederik, a gentle and urbane man, made sure his daughters had an untroubled, happy childhood*

👑 *After a visit to Greenland, Queen Ingrid and her daughters posed in the country's national costume*

👑 *In 1956, as she did every winter, the Queen took her daughters to Norway for a skiing holiday*

MON REPOS

The elegant villa of Mon Repos, just south of Kerkira on the Ionian island of Corfu, was the favourite retreat of generations of Greek Kings. Built for a British Governor of the islands in 1831, it passed to the Greek monarchy when Queen Victoria ceded the islands to Greece in 1862. The Duke of Edinburgh was born in the villa in 1921

Rex

Popperfoto

Rex

Rex

♛ Mon Repos was closed when the monarchy was abolished. Its Regency features, such as the wide, colonnaded front porch *above left* have become overgrown as the sub-tropical gardens have run riot. In happier times *above*, Constantine and Anne-Marie walked the balustraded terrace, with its magnificent views across the cobalt-blue bay to twin wooded islets. The classical proportions of the villa, with its fluted Ionic columns in white stone *right above*, contrast with the abundant greenery of the gardens, where spiked palms, cypress and wisteria luxuriate

♛ On the landward side, the gardens are more formal, with oleander bushes growing on sculpted green lawns *left*, while the brick and stucco outbuildings, roofed with red pantiles, have a more Mediterranean air *right*. Ever since the closure of the villa, the local inhabitants, the Corfiotes, have been trying, without success, to get the gardens reopened as a tourist attraction

Rex

BLOSSOMING ROMANCE

CONSTANTINE AND ANNE-MARIE FELL IN LOVE AT A TENDER AGE. BOTH ROYAL FAMILIES WERE DELIGHTED BUT THERE WAS CONCERN THAT A PRETTY DANISH GIRL WAS TOO YOUNG TO BE QUEEN OF A FOREIGN COUNTRY

B Y 1960, CONSTANTINE HAD BECOME THE very picture of an eligible young bachelor. He was lively, humorous and had inherited his father's rangy good-looks. In addition, he shared King Paul's love of sports and games, both mental and physical. Constantine was a fine chess player and had enjoyed many games with the Yugoslav Premier Tito, when he visited his Greek neighbours on Corfu. The Crown Prince was also highly skilled at karate and, in the course of his military training, had gained a fourth degree black belt.

Above all, Constantine became a devotee of sailing. This had long been a hobby of Paul's and, indeed, competitive sailing had only survived as a serious sport in Greece because of the King's intervention. Tino was soon to outstrip his father's skills at seamanship.

In 1958, Constantine was given a Lightning-class racer as a Christmas gift while, for his coming-of-age, the Greek navy presented him with a Dragon-class vessel. The speedy racing yacht had been built to a Danish design. It suited Constantine perfectly and he decided to enter it in the Olympic Games in Italy in 1960. For the next twelve months, every spare moment was devoted to practice. Constantine managed to squeeze lengthy training sessions into his schedule, mostly in the early hours of the morning, so that his studies would not be affected.

The Olympic champion

The Olympic finals were held in the Bay of Naples and, in the final event, Constantine was pitted against an Italian, who was cheered on wildly by his home crowd. Despite this, Tino swept to victory, as his parents watched proudly from the *Polemistis*, a converted minesweeper which had been pressed into service as a Royal yacht and a base for the

♛ *Constantine inherited a love of sailing from his father, King Paul. He was often to be found in the ports and marinas of Greece, where he cut a dashing figure at the helm of his yacht* above

♛ *The young Prince was one of Europe's most eligible bachelors, and his name was linked with most of Europe's young royals. The Princesses Birgitta, Desirée and Margaretha of Sweden met Constantine when they visited Corfu in 1959* above. *The 21-year-old Desirée was spoken of as a possible bride*

♛ *Constantine did not confine himself to Royal company. He was often seen escorting the young Greek actress, Alice Vouyouklaki* right, *around Athens in the late 1950s*

♛ *What had begun as a private passion became a public triumph when Constantine returned from the 1960 Olympics with a yachting gold medal. The Greek people thronged the streets of Athens in welcome* far right

Greek team. The entire family joined in the celebrations. Carl, a cousin of the Crown Prince, leapt fully-clothed into the water and swam across to Constantine's boat with a bottle of champagne. Princess Sofia turned a hose on her brother, soaking him to the skin, while Paul fulfilled an old sailing tradition and helped to toss the new Olympic champion back into the bay.

In the publicity that followed this remarkable victory, it was inevitable that the Press would start to speculate on potential marriage partners for this handsome young prince. Constantine was known to enjoy the company of young ladies and was what the Greeks call a 'loose cannon.' But he disliked nightclubs, preferring parties and gatherings at the homes of his friends, or dining at tavernas. Because of this, the gossip writers found it difficult to speculate about romance with any certainty. In fact, they were too late, for Constantine had already met his future bride.

Hellenic-Danish connections

The romance between Tino and Anne-Marie began to blossom at an early age. The two youngsters first met in Copenhagen, when Anne-Marie was just 13. The Greek Royal Family were on an official visit to Denmark and, as a treat, the children were taken to the circus. With amazing prescience, King Paul leaned across to his wife and pointed out Anne-Marie. 'Look, she is like a butterfly. I hope Tino will marry her one day.'

It took a little while for the spark of attraction to ignite. Anne-Marie admitted later that, on that first occasion, she had regarded Constantine, her third cousin, as just one more relative and was certain that he had felt the same way about her. However, there is a saying that one wedding makes another and so it proved in this case.

The happy chain of events was set in motion by the marriage of the Duke of Kent and Katherine Worsley in June 1960. During

World News, Athens

OLYMPIC   CHAMPION

Constantine's victory in the 1960 Olympics in Rome was a remarkable achievement. His gold medal in the sailing competition was the first to be won by any Greek sportsman for almost half a century and only the second to have been brought home since the Olympic Games had been revived in 1896. After Olav of Norway, Constantine was only the second Prince to have won an event at a modern Olympic Games. The people of Greece were deeply proud of their 'Olympionikis', their champion, and gave the Prince a rousing welcome on his return. Thousands of cheering supporters in Athens lined the route from the airport and Constantine enjoyed a civic reception, driving through the streets in an open-top car, accompanied by his jubilant parents

Camera Press

Hulton Picture Company

Hulton Picture Company

the celebrations, Prince Constantine phoned his parents in Athens to let them know that Juan Carlos of Spain was paying a great deal of attention to his sister, Princess Sofia. Constantine's observation proved acute. Two years later, the couple were married.

'Ideas about Anne-Marie'

It was at the wedding party on 14 May 1962 that the 15-year-old Anne-Marie and Constantine came to know each other better and realized that they were falling in love. Their mutual attraction was certainly plain for all to see. As the guests enjoyed themselves on the dance floor, Queen Frederica noticed that her son seemed to have eyes for only one person. His partner for every dance was Anne-Marie. Like a dutiful hostess, Frederica wandered across to him from time to time and chided him for neglecting their other guests. 'Tino,' she whispered, 'will you please look after the other girls?' But the Crown Prince refused with a smile. 'I'm sorry,' he replied, 'but I don't want anybody else to get the same idea about Anne-Marie as I have.'

After the wedding, Constantine was a frequent visitor to Copenhagen, where he escorted each of the three Princesses. The Press began to suspect that something was in the offing, but most journalists assumed that the Prince was courting Benedikte, Anne-Marie's elder sister. The following summer, he and Anne-Marie were both in Norway. Anne-

♛ After his first romantic encounter with Anne-Marie at the wedding of Juan Carlos and Sofia, Constantine went to Norway to race his yacht. In July, Anne-Marie left her family, who were holidaying in Jutland, and went to Norway, supposedly to visit her English governess. In fact she spent much of her time with Constantine, whose boat met hers in the Norwegian port of Hanko above. Soon after, Constantine proposed, and was accepted

♛ For six months, they kept their engagement secret. This was a difficult time for Constantine, who could only spend time with his future bride under the guise of competing in yacht races in Denmark. In January, 1963, their wait was over. Their engagement was announced and Constantine flew to Copenhagen to join Anne-Marie for the solemnization ceremony at the Castle of Amalienborg right

Topham

Hulton Picture Company

Hulton Picture Company

👑 *After the ceremony, Constantine and Anne-Marie joined their parents on the castle balcony to greet the assembled crowds* left

👑 *The demands of Constantine's official duties and Anne-Marie's schooling kept them apart much of the time. When she came to Athens for his 23rd birthday they strolled hand-in-hand through the streets of Athens* below

Marie was enjoying a holiday with her former governess, while Constantine was there to compete in a series of yacht races. They spent a lot of time in each other's company. Constantine was an ardent suitor and impetuously suggested marriage. Anne-Marie accepted Constantine's proposal with delight. He immediately told the news to his parents, who heartily approved the match. But there was some reserve in the Copenhagen Court.

At first, the Danish King was hesitant about the engagement. Anne-Marie was still at school and, in her father's eyes, too young to contemplate marriage. But there was no doubting that the two youngsters were in love with each other and eventually the King's attitude softened. He gave his consent for the match, stipulating only that they could not be wed until his daughter had completed her education and that no public announcement of the betrothal was to be made before the start of the following year, 1963. Until then, the couple were bound to secrecy.

A secret engagement

Tino and Anne-Marie kept their word and maintained a tortured silence over the next six months. This did not come easily or naturally to the Crown Prince, who complained to his family that the arrangement was 'unfair, since most engaged couples can see each other as often as they wish, while I have to sneak around, pretending that I am going to Denmark for the sailing.' These visits were, however, frequent enough for the King to remark in public that his son was spending too much time sailing. Even so, their friends were suspicious, particularly in view of the number of international telephone calls that each seemed to be receiving. 'I don't think anybody was really surprised,' Anne-Marie confided, after the announcement was finally made.

The happy news was made public in January 1963. In Copenhagen, Danish and

> *'Most engaged couples can see each other as often as they wish, while I have to sneak around'*
>
> CROWN PRINCE CONSTANTINE

Greek flags were flown together and guests soon began to arrive for a magnificent ball, held at Amalienborg Palace in celebration of the engagement. This joyful occasion brought together not only the Royal Families from Greece and Denmark, but also Juan Carlos and Sofia, who had played their part in the match.

On 28 January, two days after the ball, the celebrations moved on to Athens. Thousands of people braved the bitter cold to turn out and wave paper flags at the Royal cortège. Anne-Marie and Constantine were seated together in an open car and the procession was led by two other limousines carrying their parents. The whole city was in a festive mood. Civil servants were given a half-day holiday and a group of striking teachers voted to suspend their action and take their pupils out to join the cheering throng on the streets.

♛ *Fortuitously, the engagement coincided with the celebrations of the centenary of Greek Independence in March 1863, when a Danish Prince became King of the Hellenes. Anne-Marie was part of the official Danish party. She accompanied her fiancé on many of his official duties* above *and was much in demand at the formal balls which marked the occasion* above right. *In April the obviously happy couple went to London* left *for the wedding of Princess Alexandra and Angus Ogilvy*

World News, Athens

Syndication International

World News, Athens

WELCOME NEWS

News of the impending marriage was welcomed enthusiastically in both countries, especially as their respective Royal Families were already closely linked. When the Greek monarchy had been restored in 1863, a Danish Prince was chosen to assume the throne as George I. His father was Christian IX, a direct ancestor of the Danish Royal Family and, inevitably, the new King regularly attended the annual family gatherings in Copenhagen.

George also brought a distinctly Danish influence to his adopted country. It was he who purchased the estate of Tatoi and constructed the first Royal Palace there. In doing so, he engaged the services of a Danish forestry expert named Münter. The stables, dairy and outhouses were built along Scandinavian lines. A herd of Swiss and Danish cows was imported and the surrounding roads and forests took on an ordered, northern European aspect. Little wonder then, that foreign visitors would frequently remark how the place was the very picture of a Danish country farm.

A more durable effect of George's reign, however, was his style of government. Like Christian IX, he made his own informality the keynote of his rule. In Greece, this was essential because the people, although poor, were also proud and independent. A distant monarch would have been guaranteed a distinctly stormy passage.

⚜ *Official duties over, the 17-year-old Anne-Marie had to return to school and to family life at Amalienborg* left

⚜ *This portrait of Anne-Marie was taken to mark her 18th birthday. She wears her simple white gown with an air of sophistication. Attached to the bodice of her dress is a miniature portrait of her father, surrounded by jewels*

These precedents were given a great deal of publicity at the time of Constantine's betrothal, because Greece was in the throes of celebrating the Centenary of its Independence. George I had been proclaimed King on 30 March 1863, and, accordingly, Paul arranged an official banquet to mark this anniversary at the end of March 1963. The King and Queen of Denmark were invited to make a State visit at this time and, of course, Anne-Marie was a member of the party. Nothing could have suited the occasion more perfectly than the prospect of a new union between the Danish and Greek Royal Families.

A long wait

After the excitement of the engagement and the Centenary celebrations, life began to return to normal. The date of the wedding was pencilled in for January 1965. This meant a long wait for the young couple, but a necessary one if they were to comply with King Frederik's wishes that his daughter should be over the age of 18 and should have completed her studies before her marriage. Obediently, Anne-Marie returned to her school in Switzerland, while Constantine turned his thoughts to his official duties. Naturally, they were to see each other in the intervening period – on the Princess's 17th birthday, Tino flew to Copenhagen with armfuls of flowers to surprise her – but, even so, the agonizing separation of nearly two years must have seemed like an eternity.

As events turned out, the couple did not have to wait that long, although this was for the saddest of reasons. At the end of January 1964, doctors diagnosed that King Paul was

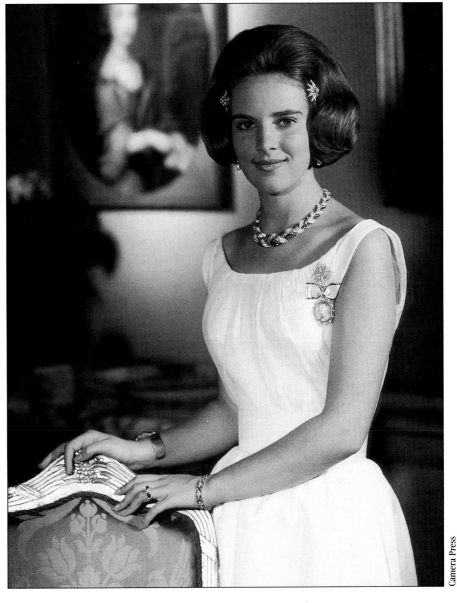

♔ *The death of King Paul at the age of 62 brought Constantine to the throne at the age of 23. At King Paul's funeral on 12 March* far left, *the gun carriage bearing the coffin was escorted from the Cathedral to the family tombs at Tatoi by an honour guard of sailors while the new King looked on, gently supporting his bereaved mother* left

THE ICON OF TINOS

The island of Tinos is a place of pilgrimage, with a reputation rivalling that of Lourdes in France. An annual procession to the island takes place on 15 August, the Feast of the Assumption of the Virgin, when a magnificent icon is paraded through the streets, watched by the sick, who hope to benefit from its healing powers. Legends about the icon have circulated since its rediscovery in 1822 when, under the inspiration of a dream, a local priest dug it out of the earth. In 1915, the icon was taken into the presence of Paul's father, Constantine I, when he was seriously ill with typhoid. On that occasion, the curative powers of the icon seemed effective and the King made a full recovery

World News, Athens

suffering from cancer. Constantine immediately telephoned his mother, who was on an official visit in New York. During their conversation, he discreetly suggested that she should cut short her stay. He did not tell her of the diagnosis, to avoid alarming her, but tried to break the news to her in the gentlest possible way. 'Papa is getting bored with the children's conversation,' Constantine said. Queen Frederica knew her son well enough to take this hint.

Death of King Paul

The King's condition deteriorated throughout the following month, although he insisted on fulfilling his most important duties. On 19 February, he managed to swear in the new government, though he could scarcely walk and had to be carried to bed after the ceremony was over. On the following day, Constantine was appointed Regent.

Surgeons performed an operation and, for a time, the King's condition seemed to improve until, on 1 March, he suffered a pulmonary embolism. As a last, despairing gesture, Constantine fetched the holy icon of Tinos, which was reputed to have miraculous powers. Paul managed to sit up in bed and kiss the famous relic, but the end was near and on 6 March 1964, the King died. News of Paul's death was relayed to the Greek people at 5 p.m. and, shortly afterwards, his ashen-faced son was driven to the Royal Palace in Athens, where he duly took the oath as the new King. His father lay in state at the Greek Orthodox Cathedral before being buried at Tatoi, alongside the other family tombs.

On 23 March, ten days after the funeral of his father, Constantine was obliged to repeat his oath as King before the 300 members of the Greek Parliament. This was a constitutional requirement and replaced the normal coronation ceremony. The occasion had an air of restrained grandeur. Constantine was driven in state from the Palace to the Parliament building, accompanied by his sister Irene, the new Crown Princess. Wearing a Field-Marshal's dress uniform, the young monarch was warmly greeted on his arrival and received a standing ovation from the deputies when he entered the parliamentary chambers. Taking his place at the Speaker's bench, Constantine listened to the brief service given by Archbishop Chrysostomos, before placing his hand on an ancient Bible and addressing the assembly. The oath itself took the traditional form, in which the new King pledged to uphold the faith, the Constitution and the independence of Greece.

An early wedding

Once these formalities were over, the plans for the Royal wedding were rearranged. In view of Constantine's new role, it was thought best to bring the ceremony forward as far as possible. The date of Friday 18 September 1964, was chosen. This would be less than a month after Anne-Marie's 18th birthday and just 12 days after the official six-month period of court mourning had ended.

There was much coverage in the Press about the daunting responsibilities that were being thrust on these inexperienced shoulders. Constantine had become Europe's youngest head of state and, already, the Press pictured Anne-Marie as a schoolgirl Queen.

There is no formal Coronation ceremony in Greece. Instead the new monarch reaffirms, before Parliament, his oath of fealty to the Constitution and religion of an Independent Greece. On 23 March 1964, Archbishop Chrysostomos, primate of the Greek Orthodox Church, provided a religious blessing before Constantine, watched by Crown Princess Irene, placed his hand on the Bible and made his declaration. Constantine's accession to the throne meant that the date of his wedding was brought forward from early in 1965 to September 1964

♛ Queen Anne-Marie at the christening of her first child, Princess Alexia *left*. The diamond necklace she wears is one that has been worn by other members of the Greek Royal Family, notably by her sister-in-law, Queen Sofia, on her wedding day when a simple diamond cross was added as the pendant

♛ Queen Anne-Marie wears the ruby and diamond leaf tiara *right*, with matching earrings and necklace, which belonged to the Russian-born Queen Olga of Greece who is seen wearing it herself on a state occasion *below right*

♛ Princess Alexia of Greece accompanied by her father *above* wears the same diamond necklace that her mother wore at Alexia's christening. On this occasion, the pendant attached to the necklace is a small diamond and pearl drop

♛ A delicate diamond necklace and bracelet were worn by the newlywed Queen Anne-Marie *above* at the annual ball of Anavryta College in Athens

Popperfoto

GREEK HEIRLOOMS

There has been no crown in Greece since 1862 when King Otho fled the country, taking the crown and other state regalia with him. When asked about his country's crown jewels, King George I, Constantine's great-grandfather, replied 'The Ionian Islands are the only jewels I bring with me.' However, George I, the Danish Prince who founded the present Greek dynasty, married Grand-Duchess Olga of Russia. She brought with her to her adopted country many of the fabled Romanov jewels, some of which passed to Queen Frederica and in turn to Queen Anne-Marie

Popperfoto

♛ The splendid tiara and brooch of emeralds worn by Queen Anne-Marie in this formal portrait *right* are part of the so-called Romanov jewels, passed on from one Queen of Greece to the next. The set is said to be worth about £2,000,000

Karsh/Camera Press

Topham

GATHERING OF THE ROYALS

♛ *Anne-Marie and Constantine emerge into the sunshine smiling, after the wedding ceremony* **above**

ROYALTY FROM ACROSS THE WORLD JOINED TEEMING CROWDS OF JOYFUL GREEKS IN ONE OF THE HAPPIEST WEDDING CEREMONIES THE COUNTRY HAD EVER SEEN

Popperfoto

♛ *King Constantine and Princess Anne-Marie pose for photographers on the terrace of Mon Repos in Corfu. Anne-Marie spent two weeks' holiday on the island with her fiancé and members of the Greek Royal Family in July 1964. The announcement of the Royal couple's engagement in 1963 took place in the year the Greeks celebrated the Centenary of their Independence. In 1863 Greece had finally thrown off Turkish rule. At the same time, a new Royal dynasty was founded by a Danish Prince. The announcement, therefore, of a renewal of Graeco-Danish links met with great popular approval*

A S THE ROYAL WEDDING DAY APPROACHED, the young couple rode on the crest of a wave of popularity. There was a great deal of support and goodwill for Constantine, a young man struggling to recover from losing his father and to find his way in a demanding role. For Anne-Marie, there was nothing but admiration. The Greek people were delighted with her pretty looks and shy manner, while the British Press recalled Queen Mary's comment that 'the women of the Danish Royal Family have the art of marriage', a reference to three of Anne-Marie's talented forbears.

A love match

Throughout Greece, there was pleasure that here was a true love match. It needed only a glance at the young couple, strolling hand in hand, to realize that this was no dynastic alliance, coldly conjured up between the diplomats of different lands.

The six months between the death of King Paul and the wedding of his son passed quickly, although they were not without their highlights. In May 1964, Constantine presided over the celebrations which marked the Centenary of Greek rule over the Ionian islands, a symbolic landmark of his country's nationhood.

Three months later, he took part in a ceremony which had a more personal meaning for him. At Olympia, in southern Greece, he lit the torch which a relay of athletes would carry, until it reached the venue for the new Games in Tokyo. Memories of his own triumph, four years earlier, came flooding back as he proudly kindled the flame.

This was the last important function which the King had to fulfil before devoting himself to the wedding celebrations which, it seemed, would take up most of September.

Before these began, there was a moment of concern. A fortnight before the wedding, the leader of the Panhellenic Orthodox Union – the ultra-conservative wing of the Greek Church – said that the service should not be solemnized, as Anne-Marie was not a member of the Orthodox faith. This was a grey area in the Greek Constitution for, although there was no legal requirement for the Queen to belong to the Orthodox Church, constitutional problems could arise if she ever needed to act as Regent while the King was abroad. The Holy Synod refuted the conservatives' argument and the incident passed off quietly.

Danish celebrations

On a more festive note, the Danish mint issued a special 5-kroner silver coin, depicting the heads of King Frederik IX and Anne-Marie. At the same time, the Greek authorities revealed that the new Queen would be receiving the Romanov jewels. These were the Greek equivalent of the Crown jewels and had been acquired when George I married Grand Duchess Olga of Russia.

Finally, on 7 September, the celebrations began to get under way. Constantine flew to Copenhagen to claim his bride and was greeted at the airport by the entire Danish Royal Family and several members of the government. Both Frederik and Constantine were wearing admirals' uniforms and, together, they inspected the Royal guard of honour and saluted the colours. During this brief ceremony, two demonstrators broke through the crowd barriers and flourished banners calling for political freedom in Greece. Police swiftly ushered them away.

The party moved off to Fredensborg Castle, the summer residence of the Danish Royal Family , for a private supper dance. On the following day, they returned to Amalienborg Palace in Copenhagen for the official inspection of the wedding presents. The climax of the visit came in the evening. This began with a gala performance at the Royal theatre, which had been smothered in flowers for the occasion, and culminated in a grand banquet at Christiansborg Castle, attended by over 1000 guests.

Farewell and welcome

On the following morning, Constantine and Anne-Marie were given a civic reception by the City of Copenhagen, which involved a splendid procession through streets that were packed with cheering well-wishers. This completed the Danish stage of the celebrations and the chief actors in the scene now moved on to the finale in Greece. Constantine flew directly to Athens, aware that he might be needed for any last-minute preparations, while the Danish Royal Family took a more leisurely route. They flew to Brindisi, where the Royal yacht *Dannebrog* was waiting to transport them to the Bay of Phaleron.

This indirect route allowed the King to welcome his bride to her new home. A 42-gun salute boomed out across Phaleron Bay and the Prime Minister, George Papandreou, greeted Anne-Marie with a moving speech: 'A century ago, Denmark sent us a young King. Now she sends us a young, beautiful Queen. We are grateful to the Danish nation for these gifts. We wish you a happy life.'

A gathering of Royals

Soon, guests began to arrive and there almost seemed to be a permanent delegation at the airport, receiving each new foreign dignitary that landed. For some, there were official events to attend – for example, a special military display in honour of the bride and groom on 14 September – but most preferred

⚜ *The love between Constantine and Anne-Marie, which so charmed the Greek and Danish peoples, is evident as he walks with her* top. *Anne-Marie was arriving in Greece for her last holiday as a Princess. In Copenhagen the Royal lovers had a chance to admire wedding presents from the Danish people* above

A QUESTION OF FAITH

One delicate question that inevitably was raised as the day of the Royal wedding drew near was the issue of Anne-Marie's religious faith. In 1950, a revision of the Greek Constitution had made it a requirement that the Monarch should belong to the Orthodox Church. However, the position of the King's consort was not specified and gave rise to some controversy. In the end, the Holy Synod, the executive body of the Greek Church, decided to avert the problem by treating the ceremony as a mixed marriage. This meant that Anne-Marie had to sign an undertaking that her children would be brought up in the Orthodox faith. A clear precedent was the marriage of Queen Frederica. She, like Anne-Marie, had been a Protestant when she married

👑 *The days leading up to the wedding saw a regular procession of royalty arriving in Greece. Princess Grace of Monaco* left *arrived looking as chic as ever, despite being pregnant. She found the heat rather too much at times. Among the many parties and balls was an official reception in honour of the Danish Royal Family. Anne-Marie arrived escorted by Constantine* right

👑 *Many of the royals took the opportunity for some sightseeing. Prince Philip, accompanied by Princess Anne and Prince Charles, toured the Acropolis* above *in Athens*

to spend the days relaxing in the sunshine.

One effect of the change of wedding date was to give it more of a holiday flavour. September was usually a hot month – it had not rained in Greece for 40 years on the day chosen for the ceremony – and, true to form, Athens was sweltering in a heatwave. For some, this proved distressing. Princess Grace of Monaco, who was expecting a baby, found it overwhelming and spent much of the time confined to her hotel. Eventually, she was forced to miss the wedding and follow the service on her hotel television. For other

guests, the heat provided an excuse to abandon protocol and behave like tourists. The international paparazzi gleefully captured shots of Fabiola and Baudouin of Belgium, strolling hand in hand through a quiet street, and other royalty, informally dressed, wandering around the ruins of the Acropolis.

One of the favourite pastimes was bathing. Constantine arranged for several of his guests to be driven to Asteria, a small private beach a dozen miles out of Athens. It was here that a slightly unseemly incident occurred.

A group of Princes and Princesses from Britain and Scandinavia had found a raft and were using it as a diving platform. As they were splashing about happily, three French photographers on a pedalo eluded the ring of Greek police boats and came close to the Royal party. 'Watch out, photographers!' cried Prince Philip. The younger members of the group swam across to the intruders and two of them – according to the photographers, it was Prince Charles and Carl Gustaf of Sweden – began to rock the pedalo on either side. Amid much laughter, all three photographers ended up in the water. It was later officially denied that Prince Charles had been involved but, in any case, it was a fairly good-natured incident.

Pomp and circumstance

The wedding on 18 September 1964 created a stunning contrast to these antics. All was pomp and panoply, witnessed by a million people on the streets of Athens and by millions more on televisions around the world.

Entire families had camped out overnight on the pavements to be sure of a good view of the newly-married Royal couple. Window spaces and other vantage points were cram-

Hulton Picture Company

Popperfoto

 *At a glittering Royal Ball on 16 September, two days before the wedding, most of the Royal Families of Europe and elsewhere were represented. Above, 16-year-old Prince Charles stands beside Constantine's elder sister, Princess Sofia, and her husband, Prince Juan Carlos*

 *Among the guests at the Royal Ball, on the evening of 16 September, was Constantine's bearded cousin, Ex-King Simeon of Bulgaria. With him is Queen Fabiola of Belgium. Prince Philip descends the staircase behind them. The assembled display of medals, decorations, tiaras and other jewellery, worn by the crowned heads of the world, was literally priceless*

'*A century ago, Denmark sent us a young King. Now she sends us a young, beautiful Queen*'

GEORGE PAPANDREOU,
GREEK PRIME MINISTER

med tight and black market prices were paid for the hire of some of the choicest spots.

The proceedings began at 10 a.m., as Constantine set off with his mother in a black open carriage, heading towards the Metropolis, the Greek Orthodox Cathedral of Athens. Dressed in his full Field Marshal's uniform, his white jacket glittering with a wealth of gold braiding and medals, he had the fairytale air of a Ruritanian Prince.

Soon afterwards, Anne-Marie and King Frederik made their departure in an open landau drawn by six greys. The Princess looked a picture of innocence and happiness.

Wonderfully dressed

Her high-waisted gown was a dreamy concoction of satin and tulle. Officially, this was described as 'in the ancient Greek style', but fashion writers insisted that it was agreeably modern. The designer was Holger Blom, Denmark's top couturier. Blom also designed the organza and taffeta outfits worn by the six bridesmaids.

Anne-Marie's decorative accessories carried a host of memories. Her veil of Bruges lace had been worn by both her mother and her grandmother at their weddings. Her simple bouquet of lilies-of-the-valley had been gathered from the castle gardens in Copenhagen, her childhood home. In addition, she wore a diamond cross around her neck and an emerald tiara, both gifts from Queen Frederica.

Inside the Byzantine splendour of the basilica, the patient guests appeared like a roll-call of international royalty. Among the company were seven reigning Monarchs with their spouses, two reigning Princes, two for-

mer Kings, two Queen Mothers and more than 100 Princes and Princesses. It seemed like a return to the days before the Great War, when the world was full of monarchies.

A candlelit Cathedral

The interior of the Cathedral matched the brilliance of its guests. Its ancient gloom was set off by the gleaming silver icons, the abundant sprays of flame-red gladioli and the shimmering light of 1000 candles. On top of this, the gold-encrusted tunics, robes and bulbous crowns of the Greek patriarchs glimmered darkly, like the memory of a bygone age. Only the clutch of microphones, set up to relay the responses, served as a reminder that this was the 20th century.

Within the confined space of the Cathedral, the heat was intense and, even in the candlelight, beads of perspiration were visible on many a Royal brow. Some must have been regretting the heavy ceremonial gear that they were obliged to wear. Prince Michael of Kent looked hot in his army uniform and Queen Frederica's osprey hat must have been stifling.

Prince Philip and Earl Mountbatten looked cooler in their crisp white admirals' uniforms, while Queen Juliana, wearing a grey dress and a large pink hat, had found the most practical solution: she had taken the precaution of bringing an old-fashioned lace fan! Perhaps the most sensational outfit was that of Queen Sirkit of Siam. Her golden gown was complemented by a huge collar-piece, studded with jewels and embroidery. She was without a hat, but her elaborate coiffure was wound into a nest for a large, sparkling gem.

The Queen was represented by Prince Philip, Prince Charles and Princess Anne. Both the British Royal children were pressed into service. Princess Anne was one of the bridesmaids and Charles, whose faintly Beatle haircut had attracted some attention in the foreign Press, supported one of the crowns in the climax of the ceremony. The Queen's gift to Constantine and Anne-Marie was a 200-piece dinner service, engraved with their personal ciphers. Other gifts must have been received with greater trepidation. Archbishop Makarios presented a silver dish bearing the inscription: 'A happy life to you and Greek Cyprus under your sceptre' – an untimely reminder of one of the most serious political threats to the Greek throne.

A Greek Orthodox service

As Anne-Marie arrived in front of the Cathedral, Princess Anne was called into action, helping to untangle the immense, 20-foot bridal train. Once inside, the 45-minute ceremony began, conducted by the octogenarian Archbishop Chrysostomos, the Primate of Greece.

Throughout the Orthodox service, there was the steady drone of chanting from the choir. In the Eastern Church, there is no requirement for the bride and groom to say 'I do'. Instead, they have to listen as the Archbishop intones the office of betrothal and the sacrament of matrimony. The first of these was symbolized by the exchange of rings and the taking of Communion while, for the latter, the service followed a Russian custom, introduced into Greece by Queen Olga, whereby crowns were held over the heads of the two partners.

Frederica's mixed emotions

Constantine and Anne-Marie gazed at each other throughout the ceremony, whispering words of encouragement. The bride's father, his hands visibly shaking, looked more nervous than she. Queen Frederica wore a more determined look. For her, the wedding was a moment of sorrow and loss as well as joy. It was only six months since, in this very place, she had made her last farewells to her beloved husband. Yet, she also had the pride of a mother, not only for her son but also for her daughter-in-law. Of the bride, she had said: 'I believe every man on earth has a star and my son's star is called Anne-Marie.'

Queen Frederica took the lead in the trickiest part of the ceremony, supporting the silver gilt marriage crowns above the young couple's heads. A succession of eight Princes took over this role in the marriage ceremony. Although the crowns were attached to golden rods, which made them easier to handle, this was a difficult manoeuvre in the searing heat.

Popperfoto

👑 *On the steps of the Cathedral, Anne-Marie and Constantine look into each other's eyes*

At one point, Frederica had to raise Prince Charles's arm, to assist him.

The new Queen of Greece

Finally, it was over. Red and white rose petals fluttered down into the nave. The bride and groom embraced their parents and Frederica made a curtsey to the new Queen of Greece.

Outside the Cathedral, the light seemed blinding and the roar of the crowd quite deafening. Spectators, who had been shading themselves with newspapers, waved frantically. Bands played, cannon boomed out and church bells rang as the couple entered an open blue landau and began the procession that sightseers had waited so long to witness.

The festivities continued at Athens Palace, where there was a sumptuous wedding breakfast for 80 people, before the newlyweds flew off for their honeymoon on Corfu.

PRINCE PETER

There was one notable absentee from Constantine's wedding. Prince Peter, a cousin of King Paul and second in line of succession to the throne, had received his invitation but chose not to appear. On the first draft of the wedding programme, Peter's name was placed among those who would take part in the ceremonial procession, but it had been mysteriously removed by the time that the revised edition was published. This pointed snub was the outcome of a protracted family feud, which had lasted over 20 years. The heart of the dispute was Peter's marriage to Irene Ortchinnikov, a Russian divorcee. By law, the King's consent was required before any member of the Royal Family could marry and, in the case of Prince Peter, this had been neither sought nor given. As a result, the Prince's wife had never been officially recognized at Court and she herself received no invitation to attend Constantine's wedding

Hulton Picture Company

♔ *A photograph of the immediate family and bridesmaids.* Back row from left: *Princesses Margrethe and Benedikte of Denmark, Princess Sofia of Greece and her husband, Prince Juan Carlos of Spain.* Centre: *King Frederik and Queen Ingrid of Denmark, Queen Anne-Marie and King Constantine of Greece, Queen Dowager Frederica of Greece, King Gustaf Adolf of Sweden, grandfather of the bride, and Constantine's maternal grandmother, Duchess Victoria of Brunswick. A clutch of Princesses were bridesmaids.* At left: *Princess Christina of Sweden and Princess Anne.* At right from the top: *Greek Crown Princess Irene, Princess Tatiana Radziwill, Princess Marguerite of Romania and Princess Clarissa of Hessen in Germany*

♔ *The scene within the Cathedral was wonderfully dramatic and colourful. The bridal couple faced a phalanx of Greek Orthodox patriarchs in their gold, red or black robes. To the sides and behind the couple were the Royal guests and heads-of-state in all their finery. The grey-bearded Archbishop Chrysostomos conducted the ceremony. Queen Frederica is seen here left holding crowns above the heads of bride and groom*

Tiara and diamond cross
from Queen Frederica

Lynne Robinson

FEMININE FLAIR

*Queen Anne-Marie has always favoured stylish,
feminine clothes, with a liking for the sunny colours
of her adopted Mediterranean country – yellows,
blues and shades of pink are among her choices.
Since her exile in England, the Queen has dressed
increasingly casually as befits her lifestyle as a
hard-working mother of teenage children*

Bruges lace veil
worn by mother and
grandmother at their
weddings

Wedding gown
designed by Holgar
Blom, Denmark's
top couturier

Bouquet of lilies of
the valley gathered
from the castle gardens
in Copenhagen

♛ As a teenage bride, Anne-Marie chose a gown
of charming simplicity. Made in white silk, it is
high waisted with inset panels of lace on the
skirt. The lace veil is held in place with a
diamond tiara; Anne-Marie's other jewellery is
the cross of small diamonds worn as a necklace

♛ The 15-year-old Anne-Marie in her Confirmation dress *right* in 1961. The white frock, unadorned apart from a small brooch, has the fashionable boat neck and wide collar of the early 1960s. Constantine was to fall in love with this slender, chestnut-haired, remarkably pretty Princess just over a year later

♛ Anne-Marie looked her prettiest and most feminine at the reception that followed her wedding. Her floating dress of white organza *left* has a border of jewel-studded lattice-work on the bodice and skirt which is matched in the loose, collarless 'cape' worn over the gown. As the new Queen of Greece, she wears a Greek family heirloom, a glittering emerald and diamond tiara and necklace, passed on to her by Queen Frederica

♛ Queen Anne-Marie with her baby daughter
Alexia *above*. The Queen wears a Greek national
costume, something she did frequently when
visiting the Greek provinces on tour with her
husband. Anne-Marie's respect for Greek traditions
and customs endeared her particularly to the
ordinary people of her new country

*The simple lines of this
outfit allow the use of a fabric
incorporating two prints: a bold
stripe and a more intricate
oriental design*

*A wide sash tied around
the hips in a large bow*

♛ The vibrant colours of
this ensemble *right* worn by
the Queen at the christening
of her youngest child, Prince
Philippos, in 1986, echo
those of traditional Greek
costumes. This was not
inappropriate since the
ceremony was a traditional
Greek Orthodox one

*Outfit topped with a skull-cap
style hat using both prints.
The hat is finished with
rouleau, and trimmed with
twisted lengths of fabric*

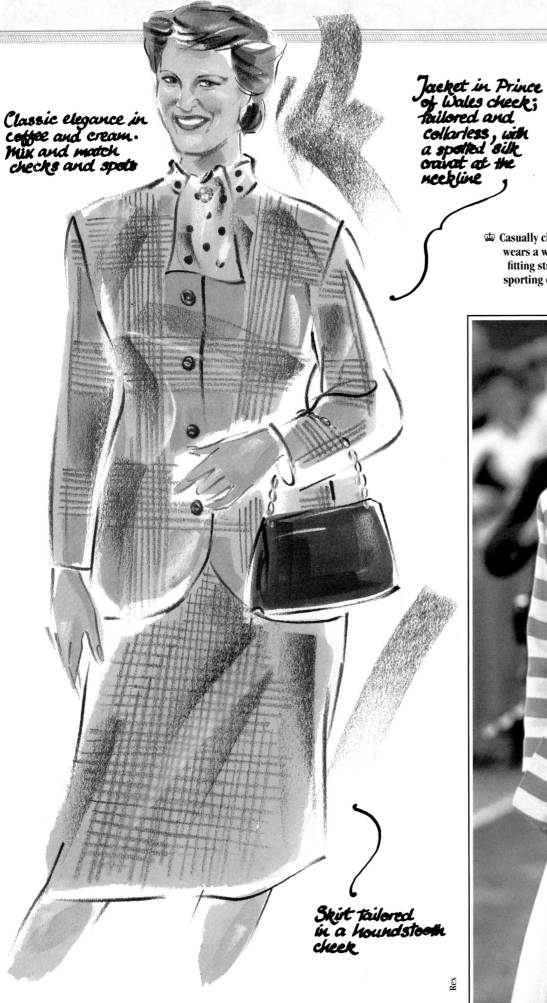

Classic elegance in coffee and cream. Mix and match checks and spots

Jacket in Prince of Wales check; tailored and collarless, with a spotted silk cravat at the neckline

Skirt tailored in a houndstooth check

Rex

♔ Queen Anne-Marie wore this smart, classic suit *left* to a fashion show in London. In recent years, the Queen has tended towards softer hues, favouring warm browns as here, and sometimes autumnal tones which certainly enhance her more mature good looks and confident style

♔ Casually chic at a polo match, Anne-Marie *below* wears a white pleated skirt topped with a loose-fitting striped jacket. She appears frequently at sporting events with her husband in stylish easy clothes like this

SIMMERING TURMOIL

THE YOUNG KING CONSTANTINE GRAPPLED BRAVELY WITH SUDDEN THREATS TO THE MONARCHY WHILE ANNE-MARIE DEVOTED HERSELF TO LEARNING THE WAYS AND CUSTOMS OF HER NEW PEOPLE

A MID ALL THE EUPHORIA OF THE WEDDING, the handsome young King Constantine and his bride may have believed that their reign would pass smoothly, consolidating the Greek people's affection for the Royal Family.

In the past, the Greek monarchy had been a precarious institution. Christian IX referred to it as 'the crown of thorns,' and George I said that he always kept his bags packed in case his subjects turned against him. He was eventually assassinated. His successor, Constantine I, was twice forced to abdicate and George II went into exile when the monarchy was temporarily abolished in 1924.

'The crown of thorns'

The honeymoon of Constantine and Anne-Marie had hardly begun when an incident in Athens offered the King a subtle warning of simmering discontent in high places.

On 22 September, even while the wedding was still fresh in everyone's mind, the government revoked a three-day-old decree by which the Greek army had been renamed the 'Greek Royal Army'. This change had been designed to align the army with the other armed services, which were already designated as 'Royal', but the decree aroused a storm of protest among government members, who pointed out that the army belonged to the nation and not to the King. The controversy passed off quickly, but it had underlined the way in which the King was caught between rival camps.

A second incident obliged Constantine to fly back prematurely from Corfu. At the start of October, Prince Peter, still angry over his wife's exclusion from the marriage festivities, took his revenge. At a Press conference in an Athens hotel, he vigorously attacked Frederica for 'spreading dissension' among the Royal Family and he also disputed the legality of the

Popperfoto

Popperfoto

ruling which placed him behind Princess Irene in line of succession to the throne. Peter acknowledged the popularity of Constantine and Anne-Marie, expressing a belief that they would 'introduce a new climate of democracy, simplicity and accessibility to the people.' But he criticized the monarchy in general for what he called an extravagance out of keeping with the poverty of many of its subjects.

Talks with the Prime Minister

A crisis was swiftly averted. On his return, Constantine had talks with the Prime Minister, who issued a statement deploring Prince Peter's attack. Although the immediate issue was dismissed as a family squabble, the row had stirred up a political hornet's nest. The cost of the monarchy was always a touchy subject and, two days later, there was an open letter in a pro-government newspaper saying, 'Prince Peter has shown us the way – let us now purge the Court to cleanse Greece.' In addition, there were fears in some quarters about Frederica's right-wing leanings and the influence she might exert, living close to the King and Queen in the Palace. Even at this very early stage of the reign, there were suggestions that she should be persuaded to leave Greece and live abroad. Frederica did, in fact, move to the estate at Psychico, ostensibly to allow the young couple privacy.

Political tension

Constantine and Anne-Marie must have been a little apprehensive as they returned from the secluded bliss of their honeymoon into this political cauldron. For both, the years ahead were to be instructive. Constantine, for all the preparations made by his father, was extreme-

♛ *Immediately after the wedding, Anne-Marie set about learning to be Greek and winning the hearts of the Greek people. On a visit to the islands of the Dodecanese the young Queen endeared herself to her new subjects by wearing Greek national costume* opposite page. *Constantine, for his part, was keen to show his bride her new country. Wherever they went, Anne-Marie was greeted with flowers* above left *and the couple were feted* above right *by enthusiastic crowds*

ly young to be a King and was bound to rely heavily on his advisers. His role was all the more testing because the Greek ruler was expected to play a more active part in politics than many of his European counterparts.

Constantine had been deeply hurt by the suggestion that he was head of an extravagant elite because he himself had little time for the glitter of Royalty. 'Even if I had the money to do it with, I certainly would not have a big fussy Court,' he said. 'I couldn't stand such an elaborate atmosphere round me. When I am not working, I want to spend my spare time with my wife and the people we like to be with.'

The King liked to rise at about 7.30 a.m. and take a breakfast of boiled eggs, toast and coffee. Then he lit a cigarette and read the newspapers. By 9 a.m., dressed in slacks and a

THE CYPRUS PROBLEM

The long-running problem which was a thorn in the flesh of successive Greek administrations was the question of Cyprus. At the heart of the matter was the Greek monarch's claim to be King of the Hellenes, a provocative title which involved jurisdiction over all Greeks, including those living in Cyprus. The quest of 'Enosis' – union with Greece, led by General Grivas and Archbishop Makarios *right* – caused considerable friction with Britain during the 1950s, when Cyprus was still a British colony. Since 1960, when Independence was granted, the main clashes have been with Turkey, bringing the two nations to the brink of war on several occasions. The island was effectively partitioned in 1974

Hulton Picture Company

Popperfoto

♔ *After their triumphant tour of the north, the newlyweds returned to Athens. The Queen, possessed with all the vivacity and energy of a teenager, made light of her pregnancy, and liked nothing better than to dance the night away with her husband at the many formal balls at which they were guests of honour* above

♔ *Life was not all play for Constantine, however. He took the duties of his position, and his political responsibilities, very seriously, and often worked a 12-hour day in his office at the Palace* below

sweater, he began official work with his small, private staff, changing into formal clothes only for holding audiences and for official state business.

Anne-Marie appreciated this informality but found the challenges of public life daunting. At the tender age of 18, she suddenly had to take on the dual roles of wife and Queen in a country that was still quite foreign to her. Despite her Royal upbringing, Anne-Marie's life in Denmark had not prepared her for such responsibility. 'I suppose I should be well-trained for this position,' she said. 'But, actually, I seemed to spend most of my time at school, so I did very little in the way of public work or appearances.'

Learning to be Greek

Her first priority was to learn the language. Anne-Marie found modern Greek, so different to the languages in which she was fluent, a

struggle and, even after two years, she was still embarrassed about speaking it in public. However, with the aid of her sister-in-law, she eventually made two speeches in Greek, much to the amazement of her husband, who had not been forewarned.

Another priority was undergoing conversion to the Greek Orthodox faith. Anne-Marie took instruction from the Palace chaplain, Archmandrite Jerome Kotsonis, and went through the confirmation ceremony at Tatoi, the Easter after she was married. Politically, this was a wise move which pre-empted criticism by opponents of the monarchy, although Anne-Marie's motives were more personal. 'I feel that I must be entirely Greek,' she explained. 'I don't mean that one should forget the country where one was born but my mother, who was Swedish, told me that when she married she immediately and consciously became part of Denmark – and that it made everything so much easier. I am doing the same.'

> ### *'I suppose I should be well-trained for this position. But, actually, I seemed to spend most of my time at school'*
>
> QUEEN ANNE-MARIE

As part of this plan, the Royal couple decided that one of their first undertakings after the honeymoon should be to tour the Greek provinces. Like his father before him, Constantine was anxious to show his foreign bride the beauties of his country. The enterprise was a great success and Anne-Marie was strongly affected by her new compatriots. 'The Greeks are so much more extrovert and forthcoming than I expected,' she exclaimed, referring to the way they would walk right up to her and ask her advice on local problems, such as the plumbing or the water supply.

Later, Anne-Marie acknowledged how easily she had settled into her new homeland. The vast majority of Greek people did their best to make their pretty young Queen feel welcome. However, aside from Constantine, her greatest ally was Frederica. She alone could fully understand the difficulties that her daughter-in-law was facing. Like Anne-Marie,

Hulton Picture Company

Popperfoto

The birth of their first child, Alexia, in July 1965 cemented the couple's happiness left. Anne-Marie doted on her daughter, whom she hoped would be the first of many children, and spent as much time with her as her official duties allowed

she had personal experience of leaving her childhood home and looking for acceptance in a foreign land.

The two women worked closely together. After her marriage, Anne-Marie involved herself in the many welfare projects which had been set up by Frederica. The older woman's support soon stifled Anne-Marie's wistfulness about leaving her family. 'I'm sure that it is because of Queen Frederica that I have never felt in the least homesick,' she said.

Work and home

Understanding the complexities of Greek politics was an altogether trickier affair, although Constantine discussed his work fully with his wife. Constantine, however, was still feeling his way in his new role and the early years of their marriage were overlaid with the troubles of the nation.

Constantine's working day seldom ended before 9.30 p.m. From then until the end of the day it took on a soothing, restful air. Friends of the couple would visit the Palace for a drink, or Constantine and Anne-Marie would listen to music and chat. 'Some soft pop music is nice, but I cannot stand noisy rock 'n' roll because it offends my ears,' Constantine has said.

Sometimes, the couple would watch a film in the basement suite of the Palace. 'I hate morbid films, but I make an exception for James Bond,' the King once explained. The Bond theme of fast cars and intrigue appealed to Constantine, who has always enjoyed detective stories and spy thrillers. He has also said that in his more serious moods, he

studied the classics of his own Greek literature.

The modern Greece over which Constantine ruled was suffering from long-term economic problems and, through his reign, there was a constant simmering threat of violence in Cyprus. Ultimately, though, the greatest single danger lay in the army. The Prime Minister, George Papandreou, was under pressure from his own party to remove some of the more right-wing elements from the senior ranks, while Constantine was equally concerned about the possibility of Communist infiltration. The crisis came in May 1965, when the Defence Minister was sacked and Papandreou

With the birth of their daughter, the Royal couple moved their family home from the hurly-burly of Athens to the more rural surroundings of the castle at Tatoi. Here, Anne-Marie spent most of her free time below, though King Constantine still travelled the 15 miles into Athens every day to his office in the Palace

Hulton Picture Company

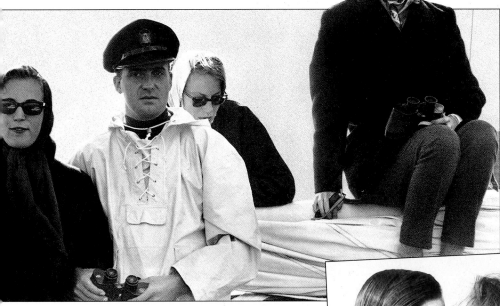

Popperfoto

often taking turns to push the baby in her pram. In this secluded setting, the cares of official life seemed a million miles away.

Moments of relaxation

During the summer, the family's favourite retreat was their villa 'Mon Repos' in Corfu. Constantine regularly commuted to Athens from the island residence and, as at Tatoi, he found that this domestic idyll provided a vital, therapeutic release from his political worries. In the midst of one of the most serious crises, he confessed to his wife that ten minutes of playing with his baby daughter made him forget his troubles completely.

tried to assume this role himself. Constantine blocked this move and, two months later, the Prime Minister resigned, expecting that Parliament would be dissolved. Instead, however, Constantine unwisely tried to form a new government from the existing Parliament and a political storm arose. Papandreou's slogan, 'The King reigns, but the people rule', was to haunt him for several years.

A happy event

At home, there was happier news for Constantine. On 10 July, 1965, Anne-Marie's first child was born, a daughter called Alexia. In accordance with Orthodox tradition, the baby was named after a saint, and Alexia was suggested by the Queen Mother. Years before, Paul and Frederica had wanted to christen their second daughter with that name but, as it was wartime, Irene (meaning 'peace') was deemed more appropriate.

Anne-Marie was very fond of children and liked the idea of a large family. During her engagement, she had worked for a time in a nursery and, even though Alexia had both a Greek and an English nanny, the Queen tried to spend as much time as possible with her. She always saw her early in the morning, before her official duties began, and in the early evening. If her busy schedule permitted, she also liked to feed and bathe her. Constantine was an enthusiastic if nervous father. Anne-Marie recounted with amusement how he liked feeding Alexia, but handed her back very quickly if she started crying.

With the arrival of the baby, the couple tried to base their domestic life away from Athens. For most of the year, their main residence was the country estate of Tatoi, some 15 miles north of the capital. Here, they would go for long walks in complete privacy,

Hulton Picture Company

♛ *Constantine still found some time to indulge his love of sailing, though lack of practice meant he was no longer the world-beater he had been in 1960. His brother-in-law, Juan Carlos, shared his enthusiasm and the Royal Families of Spain, Denmark and Greece met for a jubilee regatta in Denmark in 1966* left above. *Very much in love, Constantine and Anne-Marie lacked the traditional Royal reserve, and were openly affectionate with one another in public* left. *True to her desire to have a large family, Anne-Marie gave birth to a son, Paul, in May 1967. His christening in July* below *provided a welcome diversion from the political crisis in Greece*

Hulton Picture Company

In other respects, the social life of Constantine and Anne-Marie resembled that of any normal couple. The King retained his strong interest in sport and loved sailing and playing squash or tennis. Anne-Marie frequently joined him, although she did not have the confidence to crew for him in his boats and found that he always won at tennis. Typically for a northern European, she preferred skiing. To her surprise, she had discovered that Greece possessed a number of suitable mountain slopes for this pastime but a lamentable shortage of ski lifts.

Anne-Marie was fortunate to inherit a smoothly-running royal household. Their Swiss housekeeper was a match for her task and the only area of daily life where Anne-Marie regularly intervened was in the kitchen. Her husband was fond of good food and Anne-Marie enjoyed preparing special menus for him. Whatever happened, they always dined together, whether in the Palace or in an Athens restaurant. Sometimes they would

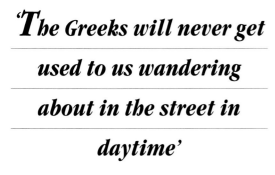

'*T*he Greeks will never get used to us wandering about in the street in daytime'

QUEEN ANNE-MARIE

select one of the large hotels but they were just as likely to wander up the winding alleyways of the old student quarter and dine in a modest taverna.

It was only on informal occasions such as these that Anne-Marie missed her homeland. 'I'm afraid that the Greeks will never get used to the sight of us wandering about the street in daytime' she sighed. 'They are so much more volatile and enthusiastic than northern races. I have found it impossible to go shopping like I did in Denmark.'

Towards the end of 1966, Anne-Marie was delighted to find that she was again pregnant. On 20 May 1967, a boy was born. They named him Paul, after Constantine's father, hoping that one day he would bring the same distinction to the Greek Throne. But a cloud was already cast over this prospect. Since Papandreou's resignation, there had been riots, strikes and demonstrations in support of new elections. The King stoutly resisted this idea and a series of makeshift governments

Camera Press

staggered on until the spring of 1967. Finally, the last of these collapsed and 28 May was fixed as the date for a general election.

The junta in power

It never took place. In the days leading up to the election, the atmosphere was thick with talk of conspiracy: a general's plot, a Communist plot, a CIA plot. In the end, it was a group of colonels who made the decisive move, instituting a coup d'état on the morning of 21 April 1967.

Soon, there were rumours that the King was under house arrest. In fact, as soon as he heard of the coup, Constantine left Anne-Marie safe at Tatoi and drove to Athens where he was met by the leaders of the uprising. Although appalled at the overthrow of democracy, Constantine saw no option but to cooperate if bloodshed was to be avoided. Reluctantly, he agreed to swear in five members of the junta. If was a fateful decision. The Greek monarchy had taken the first step towards its own extinction.

♔ The domestic tranquility enjoyed by Constantine and Anne-Marie was in marked contrast to the political upheavals of Greece. An election called for the spring of 1967 was pre-empted by a military coup. Greece was taken over by a junta headed by a triumvirate of colonels above, left to right Stylianos Pattakos, George Papadopoulos and Nikolaos Makarezos

♔ Constantine felt he had to recognize the new military regime below to avoid a civil war. Opponents of the junta, however, would never forgive him for what they saw as his eagerness to cooperate with the enemies of democracy

World News, Athens

PAST AND PRESENT

Although King Constantine and Queen Anne-Marie have lived 23 years in exile, many of their fondest memories are those of their youthful, carefree years in Greece. Exile, however, has had its advantages. The Greek Royal Family has been allowed to live a relatively normal life, and Constantine and Anne-Marie have taken a special delight in their children, whose progress has been lovingly recorded

Constantine's love for his country shone through when he escorted his teenage fiancée on her visit in 1964. He wanted to show her everything, from the remote villages in the wild mountainous areas of the North to the abiding relics of Ancient Greek civilization in Athens. As it is for many lovers, their visit to the Acropolis *above* was a highlight of the trip

👑 In 1973 the couple exchanged their life among the ancient splendours of Rome for the more serene and settled surroundings of the Surrey countryside *left*. There, they set about providing a comfortable and loving home for their family while Constantine awaited the call to return to his homeland, a dream he has vowed never to surrender. The Christmas card the family had printed in 1975 *above* shows them in front of the fire in their new home playing backgammon, a favourite game of the Greeks

Colin Davey/Camera Press

Hulton Picture Company

Hulton Picture Company

♛ *A great consolation during the years in exile has been the support and friendship of the British Royal Family. Queen Elizabeth II gladly took on the duties of godmother when Princess Theodora, Anne-Marie's fourth child and the first of her 'second family', was born in 1983*

♛ *All five of Constantine and Anne-Marie's children below speak Greek as well as English. The King helped to set up a Greek school in London for the children of expatriates. The two youngest children, Theodora and Philippos, attend the school and live at the family home in Hampstead, while their older brothers and sister are beginning to make their way in the world. Alexia works as a teacher in East London, while Paul, after three years in the army, is set to enter university in America. Nikolaos is also a university student*

Evening Standard | CLOSING PRICES

WEATHER:
Dry, fine
Lighting-up time:
9.37 pm
Details—Back Page.

London: Friday June 1 1973   3p

Premier talks of 'party of murderers'

GREEK KING 'IN PLOT' LOSES CROWN

KING WITHOUT A THRONE

IN EXILE, CONSTANTINE AND ANNE-MARIE REMAINED LOVING PARENTS, KEEPING THEIR SORROWS PRIVATE AND SETTLING QUIETLY IN ENGLAND. POLITICAL INTRIGUE WRECKED THEIR MONARCHY BUT NOT THEIR LOVE

👑 *Constantine's doomed attempt to lead a popular uprising against the junta was characterized as a communist plot by the colonels* above. *The Royal Family were forced to flee their base in Northern Greece, arriving at Rome's Ciampino airport in the early hours of the morning* below *with just four minutes of fuel left. Just two weeks later, the stress of their flight led the young Queen to enter hospital* below right, *where she miscarried*

T HE MONTHS FOLLOWING THE COUP WERE a testing time for Constantine and his young Queen. The first priority was to avoid a repetition of the bitter civil war that had torn the country apart after World War II. But the King made it plain that he saw the military junta as an unwelcome interim government.

Once the immediate furore had died down, Constantine and Anne-Marie made a tour of northern Greece, drumming up support for their democratic views. The couple still enjoyed immense personal popularity and were much encouraged by the enthusiastic reception they received. Constantine felt that the young realized he was their main hope for the future.

In September, Constantine and Anne-Marie made a trip to the United States. They were hoping for some positive assistance from President Lyndon Johnson, but left with nothing more than moral support. Worse, their brief visit was marred by demonstrations.

Anti-Royalist demonstrations
The young couple had been used to warm welcomes wherever they travelled but, this time, they were greeted with hostility. In New York, the Greek actress Melina Mercouri staged a dramatic publicity stunt, interrupting the King's meeting with the Secretary-General of the United Nations. Constantine smiled benignly, but more demonstrations greeted the Royal couple when they moved to Canada. A crowd of 40,000 expatriate Greeks waved placards and handed in a petition, while demonstrators staged a tableau in which a blonde girl – representing Democracy in Greece – was chained to a float and beaten by three uniformed men. Security men shielded

Camera Press

Constantine and Anne-Marie from the worst of these scenes, but the incident stung. On their return to the US, Constantine snapped 'It's not my government' to a critical Senator.

A Royal initiative

His attempt to reverse the coup followed less than three months later. It was a courageous move. Constantine was concerned for the safety of his family, especially as Anne-Marie was pregnant once more. Accordingly, on 13 December 1967, the entire family left Tatoi with him and flew to Kavalla in northern Greece, which he had chosen as his headquarters. There, Constantine made a radio broadcast calling for support. Unfortunately, the transmitter was weak and his proclamation was barely audible in Athens. Initially, there was support from the navy and the air force but the army, by and large, remained loyal to the junta. As the day wore on, it became apparent that the Royal initiative had failed. In the early hours of 14 December, Constantine admitted defeat and flew out with his family from Kavalla airport.

Defeat and exile

At 4 a.m., the sad Royal party arrived at Ciampino military airfield, near Rome. It had been pouring with rain when they left and the travellers looked bedraggled and tired. Constantine, pale and unshaven, blinked back tears as a barrage of Press photographers surged forward. He was still wearing his army uniform and carried a military baton in one hand while, with the other, he protectively clutched the hand of the two-year-old Princess Alexia. Anne-Marie, wrapped in a heavy fur coat to guard against the chill night air, looked distraught as she followed him out of the plane. Behind them, a nurse was carrying the baby Prince Paul. Their luggage – just nine small suitcases – made a pathetic sight as it was wheeled across the tarmac. In fact, they had packed so rapidly and in such secrecy that they had forgotten to include any baby clothes. Nothing could have made a sorrier contrast to their glorious wedding than this forlorn retreat into exile.

Constantine and Anne-Marie settled down to life in exile in Italy. Constantine wished to be near his people so that he could answer swiftly any call to return. In the meantime, a noticeably thinner Anne-Marie sought solace in shopping trips to Rome left *and in setting up home in a villa on the outskirts of the city* below. *Queen Frederica had her own home nearby*

Camera Press

REFERENDUM ON ROYALTY

The system of conducting referendums on the existence of the monarchy is long established in Greece. There have been six since 1833, with the verdict going three times each way. In Constantine's lifetime, there have been three of these crucial ballots. The first, coming in 1946, restored his uncle to the throne, while the other two, occurring during his own reign, both went against the monarchy. The plebiscite of 1973 was highly controversial, with widespread accusations that the result had been stage-managed by the junta. Accordingly, the democratic government which came to power in the following year ordered a new referendum to decide the issue once and for all. The government remained strictly neutral during the campaign and the result, showing 69 per cent of Greeks opposed to the King's return, was greeted with jubilation *right*

Camera Press

Hulton Picture Company

The Royal party moved into the VIP lounge, where they ordered tea, milk and biscuits and waited until a police escort was arranged for them. Their arrival had been so unexpected that nothing was prepared. Eventually, a black Lincoln limousine arrived on the tarmac and ferried them away to a much-needed rest.

For the next few days, Constantine, Anne-Marie and Princess Irene stayed at the Greek Embassy in Rome, while Frederica and the children took shelter in the Villa Polissena, a private house belonging to a cousin, Prince Heinrich of Hesse. At this stage, the King was hoping to negotiate a speedy return to Greece. However, once it became clear that their stay in Italy might be lengthier than expected, he rented the Villa Olgiata, which lay 15 miles outside the city.

Tension in Rome

The rest of December 1967 was a nightmare. Cameramen hounded the family everywhere and the whole family felt the strain of leaving their home, friends and country. Christmas, at least, provided a welcome novelty. In the Eastern Church, Epiphany was the more important celebration. Anne-Marie was determined that the children should not suffer unduly through the predicament and, on Christmas Eve, reporters spotted her and Irene shopping for toys and other presents in the centre of Rome.

However, the festivities soon turned sour,

♛ *In 1973, despairing of returning to Greece, Constantine and Anne-Marie decided to leave Italy, whose strong Republican tradition and history of political instability made it unsuitable for a Royal Family in exile. To return to Denmark would have entailed a loss of face for Anne-Marie, and the couple settled on England, moving first to a suite at Claridges in Mayfair* above

FREDERICA — A CONTROVERSIAL QUEEN

One of the crucial figures during the crisis of the Greek monarchy was Constantine's mother, Queen Frederica *right*. Born in Germany, a granddaughter of Kaiser Wilhelm II, and educated in England, she was an energetic and courageous woman who won praise for her welfare work, in particular the 'Relief Fund' which she set up after World War II. But her critics never forgave Frederica for her German background and condemned her for her extravagance, and for what they saw as interference in political affairs. These criticisms mounted after King Paul's death and many felt that her influence over her son led the monarchy into difficulties. Sensitive to this complaint, Frederica made an effort to distance herself from politics after the coup in 1967. She lived in exile in Italy, wrote her autobiography, and later studied philosophy in India. Even after the formal abolition of the Greek monarchy, she remained apart from Constantine, not wishing to jeopardise his chances of regaining the throne

Popperfoto

Colin Davey/Camera Press

Hulton Picture Company

👑 *In 1974 the growing family, including Prince Nikolaos, who had been born in Italy, moved to a country house near Chobham in Surrey* left, *where they stayed for two years*

👑 *After nearly 14 years of exile, Constantine made an emotional return to Greece to attend his mother's funeral at Tatoi. The aircraft touched down in the precincts of the former Royal estate and Constantine, first down the steps, fell to his knees to kiss his native soil*

as the Queen fell ill. She spent Christmas Day in bed and her doctor announced that there were fears for her pregnancy. Her condition appeared to improve over the next two days until, on the evening of 28 December, she was rushed to the Villa Claudia clinic, on the outskirts of Rome, where she suffered a miscarriage. Constantine remained by her side during the night, sleeping on a divan at the clinic. Next day, Dr Coutifaris, Anne-Marie's personal gynaecologist, released a bulletin which stated the Queen's health had been adversely affected by the emotional stress of 'fifteen tormented days' since their flight from Greece.

Meanwhile, negotiations continued with the military régime in Greece. The junta was careful not to distance itself too far from the King. His presence had legalized the original coup and, without him, there was renewed concern about foreign recognition. Thus, it was proclaimed that the monarch had 'voluntarily abstained' from his duties and was welcome to return at any time.

A call for democracy
Constantine responded swiftly. I am prepared to return to Greece. I want to return to Greece . . . I set only one condition . . . that the government announce a firm and complete timetable for the re-establishment of a normal, democratic political life. Unfortunately, he had no power to make conditions. The US Administration accepted the reality of the junta and, gradually, other powers followed their lead.

As the early months of 1968 went by, Constantine and Anne-Marie felt trapped in limbo. The longer they were away from Greece, the less likely it seemed that they would ever return. One by one, the trappings of Royalty were removed from their homeland. The King's traditional New Year Message was relegated to a back page in the national Press and censored, omitting the crucial sentence: 'We Greeks believe that freedom and democratic rule are more precious than life itself.'

'*I am prepared to return to Greece. I want to return to Greece*'

KING CONSTANTINE

In February, there was another poignant reminder of what had been lost. Anne-Marie's elder sister, Benedikte, was married in the small 18th-century chapel of Fredensborg Castle, 25 miles to the north of Copenhagen. It was a happy and majestic occasion, crowned by a procession through the streets of Fredensborg with 1,400 torch-bearing Girl Guides lining the route. Yet, it also reunited many of the people who had been present at the Athens wedding and must have stirred a few painful memories.

Hulton Picture Company

♔ *Although the Greek Government permitted Constantine's return for Frederica's funeral, they made sure that it would not be in any way a state occasion. Only family members were permitted to attend above, and Constantine had to leave the country almost immediately after the service*

♔ *The family were treated with more ceremony in their adopted home, Britain. The christening of their fifth child, Philippos, in 1986 right was attended by two Kings, including Constantine's brother-in-law, Juan Carlos of Spain, three Queens and 25 Princes. The Duke of Edinburgh represented the British Royal Family*

A more bizarre ceremony was celebrated three months later in May 1968, when the leaders of the junta took part in the traditional festivities marking Constantine's name-day. Gun salutes were fired, flags were raised and members of the government attended the traditional church service. But the Greek King and Queen were absent. Officials were shocked when the event turned into a Royalist

demonstration. Outside the Cathedral, supporters waved pictures of Constantine and Anne-Marie and chanted 'Bring back the King.' Clearly, the young couple retained a great deal of their popularity.

Final defeat and permanent exile

In view of this, the military régime held back their anti-royalist measures. The new Constitution of November 1968 limited the King's powers but stopped short of abolishing the monarchy. In fact, the junta achieved this aim only in 1973 when, using an abortive naval mutiny as a pretext, it stripped the King of his remaining rights, cancelled his allowance (Constantine had been receiving £6,000 a month out of the annual £260,000 civil list allowance) and threatened to confiscate the Royal estates.

After these moves, Constantine and Anne-Marie decided to leave Rome and settle permanently in England. The main purpose of staying in Italy had been to keep close to Greece. Their third child, Prince Nikolaos, had been born in Rome on 1 October 1969. By 1973, following the abolition of the monarchy, the King's hopes of resettling his family in Greece were fading away.

Their first English home was in Stanners Hill, near Chobham. There, they purchased

Popperfoto

Anwar Hussein

Tim Graham

the impressive mansion of 'Stanyards', built in 1883 and set in seven-and-a-half acres of land in the heart of the Surrey stockbroker belt. In 1976, they moved closer to central London, settling in a comfortable, 10-bedroomed town house in Hampstead Garden Suburb.

For a brief while, Constantine and Anne-Marie must have believed that their time in England would be cut short. In 1974, democracy was restored in Greece and the incoming government conducted a referendum to decide on the position of the King. Constantine was optimistic of success and made a moving speech, in which he affirmed his contempt for the junta and argued that the monarchy was the symbol of Greek unity. However, the voting came out in favour of a republic and Constantine accepted that his exile was permanent.

Queen Frederica's funeral

In fact, the only occasion on which he has returned to Greece since the coup was for the funeral of his mother. In February 1981, Frederica died after a routine eye operation in Madrid, where she had been visiting King Juan Carlos and Queen Sofia. Surprisingly, the Greek government agreed to her burial in the Royal graveyard at Tatoi. It may be that the authorities believed royalist sympathies would have abated over the years. If so, their illusions were to be swiftly dispelled.

The government had imposed severe restrictions on the funeral. It was to be a private family ceremony and Tatoi was cordoned off

♛ *Constantine maintained his interests in sport, enthusiastically taking up clay-pigeon shooting* above left *in addition to his sailing. Both he and Anne-Marie are in demand at shoots, horse-trials and sailing events when they mingle with the crowds* above *and are often called upon to present prizes*

to prevent any crowds gathering. No government ministers attended the service and, most heartless of all, Constantine and Anne-Marie were permitted to be in Greece for only a few hours and were forbidden to stay overnight. In fact, the stringency of these conditions backfired on the government, increasing popular sympathy for the monarchy.

The funeral was a highly-charged affair. As Constantine decended from his plane, he fell to his knees and kissed the Greek soil. Later, at the graveyard, one exuberant group of young supporters seized Frederica's coffin and carried it to the church, while another lifted the former King shoulder high and carried him triumphantly. Throughout the service, Royalist songs and anti-government slogans were chanted until Constantine urged the demonstrators to be quiet.

LIFE IN BRITAIN

Little has since changed. In 1987, the Greek government finally carried out its threat to dispossess the monarchy of much of its property, leaving it only a fraction of the Tatoi estate, including the Royal graveyard. Constantine and Anne-Marie, meanwhile, live quietly in England. Their family has grown during their years in exile. Their two youngest children were born in London, Princess Theodora in 1983 and Prince Philippos three years later.

Where possible, they maintain a low profile although, naturally, they make an appearance on important Royal occasions. Their links with the British Royal family, always close, have been increased by their friendship with the Prince and Princess of Wales. Both couples share the same sporting interests. Constantine accompanied Diana to the Wimbledon semi-finals shortly before her wedding while, at the previous Cowes Week, Anne-Marie watched as her husband tried sail-boarding with Prince Charles and Prince Edward. It came as no surprise that Constantine was chosen as one of Prince William's godparents.

In 1989, Constantine and Anne-Marie celebrated their silver wedding anniversary. Their marriage has steered them through a trail of adversity that even the gloomiest forecaster would not have dared to predict. Yet, they remain happy and together and, given the ever-changing face of Greek politics, they believe there is always a glimmer of hope that they will return to the throne of Greece.

Camera Press

Anwar Hussein

👑 *In June 1990, Constantine celebrated his 50th birthday with a glittering party at Spencer House in St James's, London* above. *The 650 guests included the Royal Families of Britain, Spain, Holland, Norway, Denmark, Sweden and Belgium as well as fellow-exiles King Michael of Romania and Crown Prince Reza of Iran*

👑 *Both Constantine and Anne-Marie maintain strong links with the British Royal Family* left. *Queen Elizabeth II is godmother to Anne-Marie's younger daughter, Theodora, while Constantine is godfather to Prince William*